Wake Up!

PALMETTO
PUBLISHING
Charleston, SC
www.PalmettoPublishing.com

Copyright © 2024 by Michele Luckey

All rights reserved

No portion of this book may be reproduced, stored in a retrieval system, or transmitted in any form by any means—electronic, mechanical, photocopy, recording, or other—except for brief quotations in printed reviews, without prior permission of the author.

The Holy Bible, King James Version (KJV)
New King James Version (NKJV). Copyright 2004, 2007 by Life Application Study Bible, Tyndale House Publishing.
Scripture quotations marked NIV are taken from the Holy Bible, New International Version (NIV). Copyright 2020, 2021, 2022 by You Version Bible App.com by Life. Church Operation LLC.
Scripture quotations marked AMP are taken from Amplified Bible. Copyright 2020 by You Version Bible App.com by Life. Church Operation LLC.

Paperback ISBN: 979-8-8229-4926-3
eBook ISBN: 979-8-8229-4927-0

Wake Up!

*Encouraging messages of inspiration
to fuel your day*

Michele Luckey

Acknowledgments

I first would like to thank God. *"If it had not been for God who was on my side, I don't know where I would be."* Some may say this as a cliché, but it is real and true to me. I have realized through my life trials, tribulations, and experiences, it has always been God who has been faithful and true in my life. God has brought me through good times and bad times *(a lot of bad times),* and because of Him, I am so grateful and thankful for His love that covers me and compassion that keeps me. I would not be the woman, wife, mother, daughter, and grandmother I am today if it wasn't for God. Thank you, Father.

To my wonderful husband, (Bishop) David Luckey Jr., married for thirty-six years: I thank God for you. I thank you, honey, for loving me the way you do; you have always been my biggest supporter. You have always supported me in all my endeavors no matter what they were, and your faith in me means so much more to me than you will ever know. David, you have always seen more in me than I have seen in myself, and you always pushed me out of my comfort zone. More importantly, you have always encouraged me to pursue my dreams and passions. I love you...more.

To my wonderful children—Shamara P., Charrisse D., and David III—and to my seven grandchildren—Sarai, Anaya, Mya, Donte, Rosalyn, Corinne, and Avery—you are my delight. I love you all very much, and I thank God for allowing me to be your mother and grandmother. I am very proud of all of you. Love, Mom and Me-Mom.

Table of Contents

Acknowledgments   v

Introduction   1

Chapter 1: When Life Deals You a Bad Hand   3
   Dealing with Unexpected Difficulties   4
   Dealing with Conflict   6
   Dealing with Challenges   8
   Your Difficulties Can Serve God's Plan   10

Chapter 2: Putting Faith into Action   13
   Speaking Faith Words into Your Future   14
   Living Life in Faith, Not Fear   17
   Having Now Faith   19
   Choose Faith Despite of the Facts   21
   Going from Believing to Expecting   23

Chapter 3: The Pruning Process   25
   Pruned for Promotion   26
   You Are Coming Out   29
   Winning the War Within   31
   Worry Adds No Value to Your Life   33

Chapter 4: Finding Yourself 35
   Finding Your Worth in Jesus 36
   Finding Your Place of Blessing 38
   You Are a Victor, not a Victim. 40
   You Are Stronger Than You Think 42
   Your Promise Is Coming 44

Chapter 5: Let Go and Let God 47
   Forgiving and Letting Go 48
   Letting God Be Involved in Your Everyday Life 50
   Learning to Move Forward When Life Is Unfair 52
   Letting Your Light Shine 54
   Keep Your Joy 56
   Moving Forward 58
   You Are God's Work of Art 60

Chapter 6: You Are a Champion 63
   The Pursuit of Happiness 64
   No More Excuses 66
   Faith under Construction 68
   Your Blessing Is Already Inside You 70
   Starting Your Day with God on Your Mind 71
   You Are Treasured 73

Chapter 7: The New You   75
    Take Your Hands Off   76
    Keep Speaking Victory   79
    A Transformed Life   81
    Pushed into Your Purpose   83

Chapter 8: You Are Valued   85
    Recognizing What You Have   86
    Bringing Value to Your Relationships   88
    Put Your Reputation in God's Hands   90

About the Author   92

Introduction

During the pandemic, in 2021, there was so much going on in the world. The world was coping with a global disease and the impact to the body of Christ was tremendous. I had numerous heartfelt conversations from people that were confused and discouraged because of how their lives were turned upside down. I realized that even in my own life the need to continue to encourage myself in the Lord. I began searching for a way to share that encouragement and love with others and as a result, God gave me Morning Inspiration ministry. Morning Inspiration has led me to encourage others in the Word of God by inspiring and relating God's Word to our everyday lives. Morning Inspiration started as one-on-one conversations with others, eventually growing into a podcast, and has inspired me to author this book. While helping others coupled with my own personal walk with God, I realized the importance of starting your day with God and being inspired by his Word. Because of this, I was led to title this book Wake Up.

Wake Up is more than just a book; it's a spiritual guide that empowers you to transform your life. It's about finding the courage to face adversity, the wisdom to make sound decisions, and the faith to trust in God's plan. It's about embracing growth. Not just in your spiritual journey, but in every aspect of your life.

Each page of *Wake Up* is filled with profound insights and practical advice, providing a roadmap to a fulfilling and enriched life. The book addresses everyday topics that resonate with everyone, offering a fresh perspective on how to handle life's ups and downs. It encourages readers to apply these teachings in their daily lives, fostering a sense of peace, resilience, and unwavering faith.

Chapter 1

When Life Deals You a Bad Hand

Dealing with Unexpected Difficulties

There have been times in my life when I found myself saying, "Why is this happening to me? I am a good and kind person, and I try to treat people the way I would like to be treated." I had to learn that in life, we all must deal with unexpected difficulties. We are not exempt. Although I feel that I am a nice person and a good Christian, that does not exempt me from experiencing difficulties. It's a part of life. Even though we know that the unexpected does happen, it will still catch you by surprise, such as an unfavorable medical report, an expensive bill, a rent increase, or an acrimonious split between family and friends. An unforeseen instance—divorce, betrayal, sickness, whatever it is—can knock you down, and it can be very difficult to get yourself back up. When the unexpected happens, that's when you should expect God to show up. Expect God's favor to be upon you, His blessings to cover you, His power to change your situation, and for Him to be with you. "Never will I leave you; never will I forsake you" (Heb. 13:5 [NIV]).

How should you look at your unexpected challenges? Look at them as God positioning you to receive and be a blessing. More importantly, see yourself as a victor, not a victim. Deuteronomy 20:4 (NIV) says, "For the Lord your God is the one who goes with you, to fight for you against your enemies to give you victory." Don't give up! Acknowledge that God is in control. See adversity as God's opportunity to bless you, then God can turn your test into a testimony. Get rid of the "why me?" feeling. Difficulties have no respect of persons, meaning difficult times can and will occur to all of us at some point in our lives "First Peter 4:12 tells us that "Do not be surprised at the fiery ordeal which is taking place to test you [that is, to test the quality of your faith] as though something strange or unusual were happening to you". Continue to stay faithful because storms don't always last. You must always look at your circumstances as temporary and know that God is in control. Put your life in God's hands and leave it there. You must stay strong through the tough times and trust in God. By continuing to have an attitude of faith, God will bring you through your difficulties better and stronger than ever, and most of all, there will be a blessing waiting for you.

Thought for the Day

Unexpected events can set you back or set you up.
It's all a matter of perspective.

Dealing with Conflict

We all have experienced conflict in our lives, so I am not talking about a one-time thing. I am talking about when you find yourself in a constant disagreement or battle with someone. Have you ever asked yourself, "Why I am always in a constant battle with people in my life?" This could be a husband, wife, friend, coworker, client, parent, and so on. When I saw myself in this situation, I had to ask myself, "How do I break free from being combative?" As I began to pray and meditate on the Word of God about my situation, the Lord showed me that some of my conflicts had to do with how I saw myself. It was a blow to me that my conflicts and battles reflected the way I saw myself. I didn't want to believe it, but as the Word of God says, "and ye shall know the truth, and the truth shall make you free" (John 8:32 [KJV]). I wanted to be free, so I had to take that truth and work on myself.

Working on yourself is a humbling experience. I quickly realized that to break free from the chains in my life, I needed the help of the Holy Spirit, prayer, and the Word of God. There are so many things throughout the day that can challenge us and make it hard to keep our minds on God: the news, problems in our homes or at our jobs, disappointments, and even things just not working out. Do you face your day-to-day challenges with God's help? Try to find the good and positive in both your situations and the people you deal with. How you look at the conflicts in your life will determine how long they stay and their outcomes. Ecclesiastes 7:9 (AMP) says, "Do not be eager in your heart to be angry, for anger dwells in the heart of fools."

When you start out your day, tell yourself, "Today I'm going to have a good day. I'm not going to allow negativity and negative people to disrupt my spirit and my day." You must know who you are as a woman or man of God. When you gave your life to Christ—spiritually reborn or saved—you became part of God's family. You have made Jesus Christ both your Lord and Savior, and you no longer live for yourself. You live for God as His child.

First you must know God before you can know yourself. Your significance is in God. God knows everything about us and wants to use us despite our pasts. You are not an accident; instead, you are part of God's plan. It is important to understand and recognize who you are as a child of God. You are the righteousness of Christ. That means you are the head and not the tail; you are blessed, you are favored, and you are loved. Psalm 139:14 (NIV) says, "I praise you because I am fearfully and wonderfully made; your works are wonderful; I know that full well."

Find your significance in your environment. Find that family member to help; encourage and speak words of life to them. In addition, be productive in your local church and don't be a watcher but a server. Set a godly example and allow the light of God to shine through you. "In the same way, let your light shine before others, that they may see your good deeds and glorify your Father in heaven" (Matt. 5:16 [NIV]).

Thought for the Day

Morning is the time when you set the tone for the rest of the day.

Dealing with Challenges

Challenges can come in many forms. You cannot run from challenges; you must confront them head-on because they will follow you. You can be challenged by someone at your job, a health situation, or something personal, such as debt collectors calling you or a family crisis. We all want to deal with our challenges in a healthy and positive way. We must approach that challenge as something we want to defeat. The first thing you must understand is that the word challenge is defined as a call to fight; i.e., a battle or duel. (*Dictionary. com, version 7.2.27*). How do you face challenges in your life? Seek the Lord, search the scriptures, and seek godly counsel on how you should handle these types of situations. It's important to not become anxious if you do not hear from God right away. Keep on praying, continue to read the Word of God, and keep faith alive.

Philippians 4:6 (AMP) says, "Do not be anxious or worried about anything, but in everything [every circumstance and situation] by prayer and petition with thanksgiving, continue to make your [specific] requests known to God." Once you have done all you can do, give it to God. Take your hands off the challenge and put it in God's hands. I know that is easier said than done; however, if we are asking God to work out these challenges in our lives, we must trust God. Proverbs 3:5–6 (AMP) says, "Trust in and rely confidently on the Lord with all your heart and do not rely on your own insight or understanding. In all your ways know and acknowledge and recognize Him, and He will make your paths straight and smooth [removing obstacles that block your way]." Minimize your focus on the challenges and put your focus on God. When you focus too much on the situation, you make it bigger than it really is. Nothing is impossible for God. Allow your faith to be released. Show your faith in difficult times, especially at times when you feel there is no way out. The difficult times are when we put our faith into action. "But without faith it is impossible to please him: for he that cometh to God must believe that he is, and that he is a rewarder of them that diligently seek him" (Heb. 11:6 [KJV]).

You must have faith that challenges will get better, because nothing you are going through is a surprise to God. Unexpected problems and challenges may catch us by surprise, but they don't catch God by surprise.

Challenges can strengthen your faith and draw you closer to God; they are an opportunity for God to turn that misery into ministry. Challenges can mature you in your relationship with God.

Thought for the Day

Obstacles are what you see when you take your eyes off the goal.

Your Difficulties Can Serve God's Plan

We all have things in life that we don't understand, things that didn't work out the way we hoped. Challenges on the job, family problems, disappointments. You may have asked God about when things would turn around. You question yourself, "Why is this happening to me?" Your difficulties are serving a bigger purpose and plan for your life. Not just the good things serve God's plan; the difficulties can serve His plan also. Many of us have had bad things happen to us. Some of those things could have been caused by our own actions, or others could have wronged you. Whatever it is, God can use it for your good. Your negative experience can cause you to look toward God and lean on Him. Being rejected can cause you to experience God's love. Every door that closes on you is an opportunity for you to experience the power of God. The promotion that you are waiting for that was denied, God will open another door with a bigger promotion that is just for you. If you want to start a business, God will send the right people into your life to help you start that business. That person you thought was the right person for a relationship, God had to remove them and send you the right one.

    The Silent Season is the toughest of them all. You do not hear from God, you do not feel His presence, and the wait is longer than you expected. Silence doesn't mean that He is not at work on you and your situation. The teacher is always silent when the student is taking a test. There is a purpose in the delay. Your blessing is on the way. That job you are being overlooked for is really God developing you for a better one. God is getting you prepared for the promotion. That business you have been waiting to start means that God is getting you ready to launch your business and sending the right people to bless you. When you know that everything serves His plan, you won't get frustrated and will see your difficulty in a new light. Remember, you can't reach your destiny without opposition, disappointments, closed doors, and betrayals, so why are you getting upset at something designed to bless you?

Thought for the Day

When you face difficult times, know that challenges are not sent to destroy you. They're sent to promote, increase, and strengthen you.

Chapter 2

Putting Faith into Action

Speaking Faith Words into Your Future

Our words have created power. Whatever we say can give life or death: "The tongue has the power of life and death, and those who love it will eat its fruit" (Prov. 18:21 [NIV]). I was always taught to watch what I say. When I was a child, I did not see the big deal in the words I used and how I used them. For example, if I could not do something specific, I would say, "I can't do this. I will never get it." Finally, someone told me that my words have power and that what I said and believed would follow me.

When I became a mother, I chose to use my words to speak life over my children. I taught them to speak words of life and not death over their own lives. Send your words out in the direction you want your life to go. You can't speak words of defeat and expect victory in your life. You can't speak of lack in your life (i.e., "I will never have" or "I will never be good enough") and expect abundance. The reason is because you will eat the fruit of what you say. Don't go around saying negative things about yourself and what you are doing, as you are prophesying these things into your future.

Listen! We all think of negative words some time or another, but don't verbalize them. The moment you speak negative words, you allow them to take root. Example of negative words include:

- Things never go right for me.
- I will never start that business.
- I will never lose weight.
- I will never get promoted.
- My ministry will never grow.

Positive and life words include:
- I believe that things are going to work out for me.
- I will start that business by the end of the year.
- I will start eating better and lose weight.
- God's hands are upon me.

Start prophesying positive words into your future. Make a report of victory about your life, describing in detail all the good and positive things in your life. You want to report things like "I'm in good health;" "I have the victory;" "My ministry will reach out to the masses;" "My marriage is blessed;" "My children are blessed;" "My business is blessed."

Don't curse your future. The Word of God says, "You have been trapped by what you said, ensnared by the words of your mouth" (Prov. 6:2 [NIV]). Don't use your words to describe the situation; use your words to change the situation. Say things like:
- I have the victory.
- I have abundance.
- I am healed.
- I have the favor of God, and I am blessed.

What you believe about yourself is more important than what anyone else believes. The words of other people cannot change your future, only you can. Your positive words create images in your future, but when you speak negative things, you are feeding those negative images and allowing those images to grow. The result of speaking positive words will change your attitude, and you will start seeing things differently in your life. Your outlook on yourself, your future, people, marriage, relationships, etc. will look more positive than ever.

Before you start your day, send out a faith report to yourself. Say things like "I'm going to have a blessed day," "I'm going to do great things," or "I'm going to make a positive impact in someone's life."

Thought for the Day

Thinking faithful thoughts and speaking faithful words will lead the heart out of defeat and into victory.

Living Life in Faith, Not Fear

There were things in life I aspired to do, like go back to school, get that degree, go for that promotion on the job, or just do different things in life. I know I am not alone. Many times, I have talked myself out of things in life that I wanted. The reason we can talk ourselves out of things is because we may feel we are not qualified, not smart enough, not good enough, and don't have the courage to step out. What I have realized is that we can talk ourselves out of the very things that God has planned for our life. I had to remind myself that I am a child of God. I was on God's mind when He created me. I am gifted, talented, and empowered, and I was called to do great things.

God created you to succeed in life. God wants you to be all He created you to be. The only thing that is stopping you is you. God has given us gifts and talents: the gift to lead, the gift of organization, and the gifts of wisdom, knowledge, created ideas. You are created in the image and likeness of God. You are a created being, so go and create. Ephesians 2:10 (NIV) says, "For we are God's handiwork, created in Christ Jesus to do good works, which God prepared in advance for us to do." You are not an afterthought. You are not a mistake. You are intentional, and He has given you all you need to succeed. Don't get discouraged when the opposition comes. You are going to experience resistance in life. It could be at your job or through other people's opposition (family, boss, coworkers, etc.) You are also going to be criticized but remember that **other people's opinions of you do not matter**. You can overcome all the negativity.

Put your faith into action, not your fear. Don't walk in fear, walk in faith. Fear does not add to your life, it takes away; faith adds to your life. Fear will rob you of your strength, confidence, purpose, and destiny. You must remember, you don't have to fight alone. God is always with you, so let Him fight for you. In Deuteronomy 3:22 (KJV), God tells Joshua, "Ye shall not fear them: for the Lord your God he shall fight for you."

We have all experienced fear. The problem is not that we will experience fear; the problem is that we can't allow fear to govern our life. 2 Timothy 1:7 (KJV) says, "For God hath not given us the spirit of fear; but of power, and of love, and of a *sound mind*." As you know, God did not give us fear, so where does fear come from? It comes from the devil.

God has given us power, love, and a sound mind. Let's look at the word sound mind. What does it mean to have a sound mind? Christianity.com says a sound mind is a stable, healthy mind. A healthy mind is linked to our attitude and outlook as people. Having a sound mind means having a positive attitude about whatever you are going through, and a sound mind is not overly concerned. Having a sound mind is having self-discipline and self-control.

Thought for the Day

Don't be afraid of your fears. They're not there to scare you.
They're there to let you know that something is worth it.

Having Now Faith

When we talk to God, we are speaking to God about things we want in our future. Hebrews, chapter 11, refers to what I will call "Now Faith." Faith is for now. Faith is not for tomorrow or yesterday. God wants to do something great in your life today. You see, God is a present God. He is the great I Am. He is not the great I was, He is not the great I will be. God wants to bless you now. So, release your faith for right now.

We have a way of saying that one day things will turn around; one day we will start that business; one day we will own a home. However, faith is for now. Faith is alive and active; it is the faith you have for today. Hebrews 11:1 (KJV) says, "Now faith is the substance of things hoped for and the evidence of things not seen." Start speaking Now Faith into your present: "Today I can be healed."

"Today I can get that promotion."

"Today I will walk in peace."

When you have Now Faith, it creates expectancy in your heart. When you go through your day, look forward and expect God to release that blessing.

God will meet us at the level of our faith. Now Faith requires us to be bold. James 4:2 reminds us that we have not because we ask not. God puts dreams in our hearts. Unlock those dreams with Now Faith. Our prayers should be in the now and present:

"God, send healing now."

"God, fix my family now."

"God, send favor now."

"God, send a breakthrough now."

"God, send prosperity now."

When you pray in the now, you will get a now answer.

Thought for the Day

Faith is not believing that God can; it's knowing that He will.

Choose Faith Despite of the Facts

There are times in life when facts are not our friends. The facts will say: You are not going to get well. You can't afford that house on what you make. You can't get that job because you are not qualified. You're not going to get that promotion because you don't have the degree. If you just focus on the facts, it will keep you from your destiny. Don't let the facts talk you out of your dreams. The facts can get you to settle for mediocrity; the facts will stop you from going after your dreams.

God is bigger than man's fact. You may not see it in the natural, but God works in the supernatural. God can do what medicine cannot do. God can promote you without the credentials and the training. Don't let the facts fool you. God is not limited by this world or its economics. The real battle is taking place in your mind, the battle of faith versus fact. Choose faith, not fact. When you believe that something will turn around and you believe it in your heart, you will begin to hear that small, still voice say, "It's going to happen." God is going to make a way, but you must start speaking words of faith, such as:

"God is going to make a way for me."

"I have the favor of God."

"Healing is on the way."

"I know my situation is about to turn around."

"God, I believe your report."

There is a battle in your mind. During that battle in your mind, you will hear another voice saying what you can't do or obtain. The devil will constantly show you the facts: the fact of the medical report, the fact that you don't have enough money, the fact that you are not going to pass that test, the fact that you failed last time. Proverbs

3:5–6 (KJV) says, "Trust in the Lord with all thine heart; and lean not unto thine own understanding. In all thy ways acknowledge him, and he shall direct thy paths." You must turn off that negative part of your mind, because if you stay focused on the facts, you will talk yourself out of dreams, promises, and promotions.

In the Bible there is a story in Numbers, chapter 13. God told Moses to send out twelve spies to view the land He was giving to them. The twelve spies went to view the Promised Land, and they came back with the facts. They told the people and Moses that the land was inhabited by large and strong people (descendants of Anak), and the city was fortified with very large walls. They reported what they saw, but the truth was that God had already given the land to the Israelites in spite of the facts. What God promises you is for you, and God's promises will override any facts. You must see yourself the way God sees you: victorious, loved, worthy, valuable, chosen, blessed.

Thought for the Day

Believe in your infinite potential. Your only limitations are those you set upon yourself.

Going from Believing to Expecting

God has put dreams, desires, and promises in our hearts, but with everything there is always a time of waiting involved. Much of our time is spent waiting. There is a good way to wait and a bad way to wait. In our waiting, we must wait with expectancy. Psalm 37:7 (NIV) says, "Be still before the Lord and wait patiently for him." We all know waiting is easier said than done, but we must wait. Having patience is the key and is a requirement to receive all that you are expecting. Patience is a virtue. Patience is the ability to wait for something without frustration. It is a quality that everyone should aspire to. Patience is one of the Fruits of the Spirit (see Gal. 5:16).

In waiting, do not be negative and discouraged but wait with expectation. Waiting with expectation means that you are hopeful and positive. When you get up in the morning, you should expect good things to happen to you each day. Have the mindset that this is the day that God will turn it around. You must change the narrative from believing to expecting. Say to yourself, "This will be the day I receive my promise." "This is the day for my breakthrough." "This is the day for my healing."

Let's talk about the correct way to wait, which happens when you act like it's going to happen while you are waiting. Having the right mindset is pivotal. Prepare as if it's going to happen. For example, when you are waiting for someone to come for dinner, you don't wait until they show up to start cooking dinner—you prepare in advance because you expect them to come. Put your action behind your prayer. When you do what you can, then God will do what you can't. James 2:17 (KJV) says, "Even so faith, if it hath not works, is dead, being alone." Sometimes we can believe one way, but our actions do the opposite. When doing such things, you are preparing for defeat. Stay hopeful and positive.

There is a difference between believing and expecting. You can believe in having a baby or starting a business. Expecting is when you buy baby clothes and fix up the nursery, or locate a building, take measurements, and buy the things necessary for the business. Putting actions behind your faith will get God's attention. When you prepare, it will affect your attitude and how you think and will give you the confidence you need. When a person plants a seed in their garden, they do not believe something will grow—they expect it to grow. Seeds are dreams, desires, and promises. Time is the waiting process. Harvest is the manifestation. Psalm 27:14 (KJV) says, "Wait on the Lord: be of good courage, and he shall strengthen thine heart: wait, I say, on the Lord." Start making plans to succeed. Be on the lookout for opportunities. You can't be successful by being passive. Be a go-getter. Keep the dream and vision in front of you and go on expecting. God wants you to live a blessed life. God specializes in the supernatural; when you do the natural, God will do the supernatural.

Thought for the Day

To accomplish great things, we must not only act, but also dream; not only plan, but also believe.

Chapter 3

The Pruning Process

Pruned for Promotion

We all go through times when we feel like we are going backward. You were succeeding in your job, your family was doing well, and you knew you had God's favor. Then it seems like suddenly things turn: your job is not going so well, you are experiencing family problems, your friends leave, etc. Having difficulty doesn't mean you are not following God's will. God is ordering your steps; you are just in the pruning process.

During the pruning process—cutting the bad so the new can come—God sometimes orders a cutback. Just as there are seasons of growth, there are also seasons of pruning. Without the pruning, you will not become all you are created to be. God will not allow a cutback unless it will eventually work out for your good. The pruning process is uncomfortable. God will cut certain people out of our lives, but without the pruning, we would allow certain people into our lives that are not good for us, so God must prune those people.

God may have cut certain opportunities out of your life; it could have been a job or a promotion that you didn't get because it wasn't right for you. You may not see it, but it is all going to work out for your good. God would not have you lose some things if He wasn't going to give you something better.

God may have pruned a friend out of your life, but there may be a better friend coming. God may have pruned a job, but there is a better job on the way. Don't get discouraged by the cutback; it's a sign of new growth coming. John 15:1–2 (NIV) says, "I am the true vine, and my Father is the gardener. He cuts off every branch in me that bears no fruit, while every branch that does bear fruit, he prunes so that it will be even more fruitful."

When you have things in life that are not productive, such as a relationship or a job that is pulling you down, God will cut those things away and have you focus on things that are moving you forward. Growth requires pruning. The only way to grow from one level to another is through pruning. Years ago, when my husband and I bought our first home, I planted a few rose bushes in our yard because I love roses. I did not know how to take care of them, but a friend of mine told me that pruning is important to the health of roses. Pruning removes dead and diseased things from the rose bush so fresh and new flowers can grow. The pruning leaves room for growth and circulation.

Without the cutback, you won't see growth. You must recognize when you are in the Pruning Season. If not, you may feel that God is punishing you or that He is upset with you. Be calm—He's just cutting off the fat. In the natural body, there is what you call bad fat. In your spiritual life, God wants to remove the bad fat. Bad fat in your life will cause you to have an unhealthy spiritual walk and relationship with the Lord. You may be satisfied with where you are (complacent, mediocrity), but God is not satisfied. God loves you too much to let you miss your destiny. God has a new level in front of you, so it's time to get in shape and start trimming off the fat.

Will you trust God in the Pruning Season? When things seem as if they are not going to get better, when discouragement tries to set in, will you trust and have faith in God? The cutback seasons are all part of the process and are a sign that new growth is coming.

Thought for the Day

Every experience is part of God's pruning process. You've been picked out to be picked on. He cuts off fruitless branches and prunes fruitful ones.

You Are Coming Out

We all face situations that look permanent, such as our jobs, health issues, and relationships, to name a few. It's easy to think and accept that's the way it's going to be. Just because it seems permanent to you doesn't mean it's permanent to God. God doesn't allow you to get into anything that He can't bring you out of. Don't focus on what it looks like. He knows the end from the beginning. God had the solution even before you had the problem. It may look like your situation will not change, but God is saying that it's temporary. You are coming out of loneliness, pain, and debt. That situation you are in is not going to be permanent, and you are coming out. God already made an escape plan for you. God has already planned your coming out; it's just a matter of time until you see your breakthrough, healing, deliverance, and new level.

God is the Alpha and the Omega; He has already set an end to that situation. Your coming out date has already been established. Don't believe the negative thoughts that will come and discourage you; remind yourself that God has you in the palm of His hand and already has a set time of success, new levels, favor, and blessing for you. Stay in faith because God has your end date right around the corner. You must tell yourself, "I'm coming out," even when you don't see it or feel it. When those times come, make an agreement with God and His word. Align yourself with the Word of God. Start telling yourself, "I'm coming out of my drought into prosperity." "I'm coming out of fear and worry into peace." "I'm coming out of depression into joy." In Psalm 23:4 (NIV), David said, "Even though I walk through the darkest valley, I will fear no evil, for you are with me." David didn't say, "I'm staying in the valley." He didn't say, "I'm stuck in the valley" or "I live in the valley." The valley is a temporary place. You are supposed to go through the valley—don't allow your circumstances to become permanent in your thinking, as that will keep you from your destiny.

Thought for the Day

Success is to be measured not so much by the position that one has reached in life as by the obstacles that have been overcome while trying to succeed.

Winning the War Within

There is a battle taking place in each one of us. It is a battle between the flesh and the spirit. The flesh represents our carnal nature: jealousy, pride, and bitterness. This doesn't require discipline; you just do whatever you feel. We as believers are walking in the Spirit, the Word says: "Therefore, if any man be in Christ, he is a new creature: old things are passed away; behold, all things are become new" (2 Cor. 5:17 [KJV]). A new spiritual being means being in the likeness of God, and that is how we should govern our lives. We should strive to be kind, gentle, and peaceful, have self-control, and express the love of God to all.

You must remember that the flesh always wants to rule and have control over you. What does that mean? For those who allow themselves to live by the dictates of the flesh, the flesh becomes in control and your godly spirit decreases. Whenever you feel you want to compromise, give in to temptation, and respond in a manner like eye for an eye, you are allowing the flesh to win. When you walk in the Spirit, you do the right thing when it's hard; hold your tongue even when someone is rude and stay faithful in your relationships. The problem is not that people are not good—the problem is that they keep sowing to the flesh.

Start saying to your flesh, "I am not going to get jealous over what someone else has," and say instead, "I want the best for that person." Quit letting the flesh be the dictator because the flesh will not lead you anywhere productive. Galatians 5:16 (KJV) says, "This I say then walk in the Spirit, and ye shall not fulfill the lust of the flesh." The two forces are always fighting against each other.

Become skilled at controlling the flesh. Tell yourself, "I am not going to allow myself to say anything I want." When your flesh wants you to respond in a negative manner, don't take the bait. Don't be offended, jealous, envious, or give in to temptation. Are you winning the war within? Are you living by the Spirit and making decisions that honor God? Or are you letting the flesh win? Take the flesh off the throne and quit letting it determine your decisions. The flesh wants to stay on the throne and tell you what to do and where to go. The only way the flesh comes off the throne is if you forcefully remove it.

If someone does you wrong, the flesh will say, "This is not right. You must get back at that person." You must put your foot down and tell your flesh, "You don't control me. I have taken you off the throne. I walk by the Spirit, not by the flesh." It's time to dethrone the flesh. Don't allow it to dictate how you think, how you live, or how you respond to people who have wronged you. Start sowing into the Spirit and do the right thing when it's hard. Be disciplined, and do not give in to temptation.

Thought for the Day

I am never in control of what happens around me,
but I am always in control of how I respond.

Worry Adds No Value to Your Life

In life, you will be presented with things to worry about, such as war, health, money, family, or your job. We will always have concerns and cares, but worrying adds no value to your life. We all know that worrying is not a good thing; however, I'll tell you what worrying does. Worrying changes your personality; it makes you cranky, angry, depressed, and suspicious. More importantly, it causes you to be unfruitful in your life. Worry is defined as to torment with cares, anxieties, troubles; to throw into commotion; to stir up and disturb (Dictionary.com, vol.7.2.27). When you are worried and troubled, that allows you and your mind to miss out on what's going on in your life right now. You can't allow the day-to-day cares of this world to pull you away from God. Being stressed over things will cause you to go in the wrong direction. First Peter 5:7 (NIV) says, "Cast all your anxiety on him because he cares for you." Just throw your burdens on God and allow Him to carry them. There is nothing we are going through that we cannot cast on the Lord.

Luke 10:41(NIV) says, "'Martha, Martha,'" the Lord answered, "'you are worried and upset about many things.'" Martha allowed what she had to do to become stressful and worrisome. Mary stopped and allowed Jesus to speak in her life. She had things to do, but the fruitful thing was to spend time with Jesus. Sometimes you must stop what you are doing and take a Jesus moment. Turn your worry into prayer; take your worry list and put it on your prayer list. You can talk to God about anything. Prayer and worry can't coexist as they are opposites. Bring God into your day-to-day challenges.

Paul tells us how to win the war on worrying. According to Philippians 4:6 (AMP), "Do not be anxious or worried about anything, but in everything [every circumstance and situation] by prayer and petition with thanksgiving, continue to make your [specific] requests known to God."

Ask yourself, "Am I worrying, or am I praying?" God wants you to live in peace. Are you an overthinker? The two basic things that underlie overthinking are stress and anxiety. Remember, you can't change one thing by worrying. Matthew 6:25 (NIV) says, "Therefore I tell you, do not worry about your life, what you will eat or drink; or about your body, what you will wear. Is not life more than food, and the body more than clothes?" Verse 27 (NIV) says, "And who of you by worrying can add one hour to [the length of] his life?" Stop worrying and invite God into your life. God wants to take your heavy load away, and all you must do is give it over to Him. Worrying can choke out the things of God in your life, so don't allow the cares of life to pull you away from God.

Remember that worry is not a friend—it is your enemy. Worrying can cause health problems, mental problems, and family problems. Don't hold on to worry; release your cares, release stress, and release trouble.

Thought for the Day

Worry is like a rocking chair. It gives you something to do,
but it never gets you anywhere.

Chapter 4

Finding Yourself

Finding Your Worth in Jesus

There are so many things in this world that can and will try to steal your worth. God made us worthy through His Son, Jesus. We need to place our value, identity, and worth in Jesus Christ. So, we shouldn't put our value in things, such as our house, car, job, or title. Everything that was just named will depreciate, and they are all temporal. The enemy, the devil, knows your value is in Jesus Christ and that's why he tries to discourage you in areas of your life.

The first thing to do is not give the enemy any space in your life. Don't walk in agreement with the enemy. Don't talk down about yourself. Stop telling yourself you are not good enough, you are not smart enough, and you are not going to succeed in life. The devil's job is to make you believe that you have nothing to offer and nothing to give. That's why he spends so much time trying to get you to tear yourself down. When you tear yourself down, it deteriorates your purpose. When someone's worth and value is torn down, they feel as if they have no purpose. This is why many people feel they have nothing to give. Deteriorate means to make someone become worse or inferior in character, quality, and value. Stop looking for your identity in people, comparing yourself to others, and looking for others to see your worth. Do not look for someone to tell you how smart you are, how pretty you are, and how good you are. Stop looking around for people to build you up. ***Your identity is in Jesus Christ. Your worth is in Jesus.*** He counted you worthy when He died on the cross for you and me.

Take the time to feed on the Word of God so it can build you up, and your confidence will increase. You will not find your purpose and value in temporal things but in eternal things. Second Corinthians

4:18 (NIV) says, "So we fix our eyes not on what is seen, but on what is unseen, since what is seen is temporary, but what is unseen is eternal." The devil will try to make you doubt who you are. Matthew 4:1–11 tells the story of how Jesus was led into the wilderness to be tempted by the devil. The enemy will come through an insecure door. Jesus did not have any insecurities, but in this verse he was hungry. Jesus had fasted for forty days and nights. The devil attacked Jesus via temptation when he felt Jesus was vulnerable. The devil asked Jesus to turn stones into bread to get Jesus to use his authority for personal gain during fasting. Matthew 4:4 (NIV) Jesus answered, "It is written: 'Man shall not live on bread alone, but on every word that comes from God.'" If we aren't careful, the enemy will attempt to come in through an insecure place in your life when you are vulnerable. During challenging moments, the devil will say things like if God loves you, why did you lose your job? Or if God loves you, why did He allow your spouse to leave you? Just as Jesus responded to the devil, your response should also be based on the Word of God.

Jesus defeated the devil because he knew who he was. The enemy's objective is to devalue you. Remember, Jesus overcame so we can overcome. Remind yourself of who you are in Christ. In Him, you are worthy; you are beautiful; you are chosen, precious, and valuable. You are redeemed and forgiven; you are fearfully and wonderfully made.

Thought for the Day

When you know your worth, no one can make you feel worthless.

Finding Your Place of Blessing

There is an importance in staying in the right place. God created places before He created people. He created the ocean, then He created the fish to go in the ocean. God created land, then He created animals for the land. Places are important to God. He didn't create a bird to live in the sea; He didn't create fish to live on land. There was a specific place where God created each one of them to thrive. God has a specific location for every one of us to be blessed. God has a specific job for you to work and a specific home and neighborhood for you to live in. Your location is extremely important to God. They say it's about location, location, location. God is not going to bless you just anywhere; He will bless you where you need to be.

Your blessing is connected to a certain place, so don't pick up and leave your place of blessing. People have left jobs simply because they were offered more money, but if that place was a place of peace, fulfillment, and security, then that was your place of blessing. Throughout your life, the Holy Spirit will lead you and guide you. Begin to ask yourself, "Is this the place I should be?" God has a specific place where He commanded you to be blessed. When you are at the center of God's perfect will, there will be no struggle. The only thing that is holding you back is that you are in the wrong location. Follow your own place of blessing because your place of blessing can move. There will be times when God will tell you to move from where you are, and you will have no idea where God is moving you to, but He has a place of victory in store for every one of us, and it is up to us to get to that place.

In Genesis, chapter 12, God told Abraham to leave his country (his father's house): and assured Abraham that He would lead him to his place of blessing. If Abraham did not move, he would have missed his blessing. He and his wife, Sarah, would not have had Isaac, the child they prayed for, and Abraham would not be the father of faith. If you are not at your place of blessing, favor can't find you, blessings can't find you, promotion can't find you, and prosperity can't find you.

Thought for the Day

When God prepares the place and opportunity, choose to act suddenly. Have faith. Seize it for such a time as this.

You Are a Victor, not a Victim.

Learning not to be a victim is easier said than done. When you have experienced hurt, disappointments, betrayal, and abandonment, it is hard to feel any other way but victimized. I have learned that God has made me victorious by way of Jesus Christ. I have the victory, so now I can look at my circumstances differently and see myself not as a victim but as victorious. God has called us to be more than conqueror through Christ Jesus.

Have a Champion Mindset
A champion does not lie down easily. When you are faced with difficulties and trials, you are not easily taken out by every disappointment or closed door. A champion has a mental resilience to bounce back. Attaching yourself to the label of being a champion will give you a different mindset because your thoughts will follow your actions. Attach your mind to the mind of Christ; take inventory of what you are thinking about yourself. Are you thinking of champion thoughts or weak and defeated thoughts? Are you thinking "I can do all things" thoughts? (i.e., I am more than a conqueror; I have the victory through Jesus Christ.) Second Corinthians 2:14 (KJV) says, "Now thanks be unto God, which always causes us to triumph in Christ."

Check Your Mental Indicator
When you are driving in your car, you check your gas indicator, oil indicator, and engine indicator. They tell you how your car is running. Check your mental indicator too. Make sure you are thinking the right thoughts. Are you telling yourself positive things or negative things? Are you acting like a champion and overcoming the punches

of life? Life is like a boxer in a ring: every now and then you will get knocked down, but do you have what it takes to bounce back? Make sure you are filling and fueling your mental and emotional tank and taking care of your total being. You are three parts: spirit, soul, and body. Philippians 4:8 (KJV) says, "Whatsoever things are true, whatsoever things are honest, whatsoever things are just, whatsoever things are pure, whatsoever things are lovely, whatsoever things are of good report; if there be any virtue, and if there be any praise, think on these things."

Develop Mental Toughness

The first thing you must understand is that God is for you and not against you. No matter what you are going through, you are not alone. I have to remind myself that God is with me, that He is cheering me on, giving me the strength I need to get through tough times, and He will never put more on me than I can bear. There are many times when I have to remind myself that I am more than a conqueror.

What is a champion? A champion is their own cheerleader. A champion doesn't wait for someone to puff them up and give them a pat on their back. A champion will always speak positive declarations over their life: "I am talented." "I am enough." "I am worthy." "I am fearfully and wonderfully made." "I am an overcomer." "I am victorious." "I am the head, not the tail; above and not beneath."

Thought for the Day

You cannot expect victory and plan for defeat.

You Are Stronger Than You Think

In life you will encounter difficulty and you will feel like giving up because of the pressure, but God has designed and equipped every one of us to go through all that we would face in this world to be successful and fulfill our destiny. Second Peter 1:3 [NIV] says, "His divine power has given us everything we need for a godly life through our knowledge of him who called us by his own glory and goodness." God is your architect. When designing a building, an architect takes into consideration the foundation, the structure, how much weight it can handle, and where it will be placed. God knows every difficulty you will go through; He has even prepared you for the storm. Every disappointment, adversity, and hurt that you will encounter, God has designed you to handle it. Ephesians 2:10 [NIV]says, "For we are His workmanship created in Christ to do good works, that He prepared in advance for us." You will not face anything that God has not equipped you to go through. 1 Corinthians 10:13 [NIV] says, "And God is faithful; he will not let you be tempted beyond what you can bear."

Listen up! You are equipped with favor, power, strength, and determination. Recognize that you are a son or daughter of God and that you are not alone. God promised that He would never leave or forsake you. You are designed for what He has given you. When God created you, He created and put in you whatever you need for what you will go through. You are the right nationality, you are the right size, you live in the right place, and you work at the right job. Don't have a defeated mindset. Defeated thoughts start in the mind first. You want that "I can do all thing through Christ" mindset. Don't say "My situation will never change." Don't say, "I am not going to be healed." Isaiah 53:5 [NKJV] says, "And by His stripes we are healed." Healing belongs to you.

We have all asked ourselves, "Why am I going through this?" Jesus told the disciples, "That in me ye might have peace. In the world ye shall have tribulation: but be of good cheer; I have overcome the world." Fight for your future because I am going to fight for mine! Don't surrender to defeat—instead go after what God has prepared for you. It has your name on it. You will never know how strong you are until you are faced with the pressures of life. You are stronger than you think.

Put your trust in God. Trust says that God is in control. If you believe in something, then start preparing. You are putting your faith into action. Write the plan for that business. If you want a better job and more money, then get that resume out there. Start praying over that child. Start praying for that marriage. Start praying and ask God to send you your spouse.

Thought for the Day

You never know how strong you are until being strong is the only choice you have.

Your Promise Is Coming

We all have things we believe in, such as dreams, desires, and goals. We also have problems that we are waiting to turn around, and our circumstances may say that if it hasn't happened by now then it will not happen. It's easy to get discouraged and feel like it's not going to work out, but what God promises you doesn't have an expiration date. Don't give up on your dreams. You may have given up on some dreams in your life, but that doesn't mean God has given up on them.

Although you may have done something that has kept a dream from coming to pass, God is merciful, and He has already taken your mistakes into account. You may have delayed it from happening, but you have not denied it from manifesting. The promise is still coming, despite your mistakes and failures. Don't disqualify yourself. You may have said that it would have happened if you had made better choices such as finishing school, not getting involved with that person, not following the wrong crowd, or not wasting time. All of that would be true if God was like us and judged us based on our performance.

God doesn't cancel destiny. He helps fulfill it. Just because you got off course and made mistakes doesn't mean that you've missed out on what you're meant to have. God knew every mistake you would make, every wrong turn you would take. Nothing you have done has caught God by surprise. God has mercy for every mistake, restoration for every failure, and a comeback for every setback. What God promises is still on the way—the delay doesn't mean it's not going to happen. Stop believing the lies! John 8:44 [NIV] says, "[The devil] When he lies, he speaks his native language, for he is a liar and the father of lies." He will tell you things like it's too late; you wasted too much time; you did too many bad things in your life; God is disappointed in you. God has not changed His mind. Just because God is silent doesn't mean He has given up on you. You may have delayed it, but you didn't deny it. Trust God. Proverbs 3:5–6 (NIV) says, "Trust in the Lord with all your heart and lean not on your own understanding; in all your ways submit to him, and he will make your paths straight." The wrong voice could tell you that it's not going to happen, that too much time has gone by, but your promise is still on the way.

Thought for the Day

When you focus on God's promises instead of the problems, your thoughts will be positive and filled with peace.

Chapter 5

Let Go and Let God

Forgiving and Letting Go

In life, we all have unfair things that happen to us. We can choose to hold on to the hurt, become bitter and angry, and allow it to affect our future, or we can choose to let it go and trust God. You may think that you are unable to forgive and let go. I get it. I'm sure you have said the same things I have said to myself: "You don't know how that person hurt me." "They embarrassed me." "They betrayed me." "That person lied to me." "That person stabbed me in the back." For you to get all that God has planned for your life, you must forgive. Forgiveness is not for the other person; it is for you.

You will not be able to live in a place of liberty or freedom if you are holding on to past pain and hurt. When you forgive, you take away the power of others to hurt you. The mistake we make is that when we hold on to bitterness and anger, we allow others to continue to hurt us. Others are living their lives, going out and enjoying life, but you are walking around hurt, bitter, and unable to move forward. I've met folks who are still mad at people they haven't seen for ten or twenty years. Further, there are people who have not spoken to family members for many years. Don't let people continue to hurt you and allow you to stay angry. The Bible says in Ephesians 4:3[NIV], "Get rid of all bitterness, rage and anger, brawling and slander, along with every form of malice." Don't allow unforgiveness to ruin your life. It is not worth it for you to miss your destiny. I can remember a story in Genesis 37:1–36, in which Joseph was betrayed by his brothers and thrown into a pit. He was sold by his brothers to the Ishmaelites, and later falsely accused and thrown into prison. Joseph could have let all those things keep him from his destiny and ruin his relationship with God, but Joseph had favor with God.

God is with you no matter what you are going through. Genesis 50:20 [NIV] says, "You intended

to harm me, but God intended it for good to accomplish what is now being done, the saving of many lives."

Forgiveness is not about you excusing their behavior; forgiveness is about letting the offense go so you can be free. More importantly, forgiveness is about you not missing out on your future and destiny. So, you may ask, how do you let it go?

"Quit dwelling on it."

"Stop repeating it in your mind."

"Don't give it time and emotional energy."

"If you let it go, God will take that hurt and turn it into a blessing."

Every time you replay what happened, you open an old wound. When you don't let it go, you won't heal properly. Don't get stuck in the pain. When you are bruised, you are not free. If you want the bruise to go away, then you must forgive and let it go. Give yourself permission to be healed; it releases you to move forward.

Thought for the Day

If what's ahead scares you and what's behind hurts you, then just look above! God will never fail you.

Letting God Be Involved in Your Everyday Life

God is not only interested in the big things that go on in your life—He is also interested in every and all aspects of your life. God cares how your day goes, how you do on your job, and about your relationships with other people. God is interested in the smallest details of your life. Unfortunately, we see God only as a rescuer. God cares about what you care about; He is not a God that is so far off and removed that he can't reach you in your life. Acts 17:27 (NIV) says "…though he is not far from any one of us."

God wants you to succeed in your life. In 3 John 1:2 (KJV) it says, "Beloved, I wish above all things that thou mayest prosper and be in health, even as thy soul prospereth." God wants to help you in your life, but He will only be involved in your life as much as you allow Him.

How do you acknowledge God in your everyday life? You do so by letting God know you are depending and relying on Him. Involve God throughout your day; tell Him how much you need Him. Acknowledging God shows your dependence is on Him. Unfortunately, we have God in our Sunday box, and we only acknowledge and pull Him out when we go to church. Get into a habit of acknowledging God, and you will be surprised how well your day will go and how you will begin to see favor in your life.

Acknowledge God throughout your day. Say things like:

"God, be with me on my job, when I go into this meeting."

"Help me speak with this loan officer."

"Help me start this business."

"Help me start my ministry."

"Help me write my book."

I once heard someone say, "I don't meet with anyone until I meet with God." Give your day to God. By doing that, you are recognizing that He is your true strength.

Start your day by saying, "Thank you for waking me up this morning, for breathing the breath of life in me, for giving me the activities of my limbs, and for new mercies. I can't do this day without you. You are my strength, my confidence, my trust, and my wisdom. You created this day for me to succeed."

Thought for the Day

Good morning is not just a phrase; it is an action and a belief to live the entire day well.

Learning to Move Forward When Life Is Unfair

We all go through disappointments and struggles in life when things don't happen the way we plan, such as breakups in relationships, being overlooked on the job, or unexpected illness. It is easy to use what is unfair as an excuse for why you have not moved forward. It may not be your fault when you get knocked down, but it is your responsibility to push yourself back up. Getting up requires faith. It's easy to stay down, feel sorry for yourself, and say that the situation was unfair or that person did you wrong. When you choose to stay down, you are choosing to give up on your dreams. God has a plan and a purpose for your life, and you are bigger than what you are going through. We serve a God that sees all things.

God will pay you back and give you double for the unfair things that have occurred in your life. For example, God gave Job double of all he had lost for his trouble. That means that whatever plan God has for your life, it is much bigger and better than what you are going through, so hold on and don't give up. Don't sit around in defeat when life gets hard; don't continually replay the unfairness in your mind and shake off the hurt and bitterness. Stop saying things like "Why did this happen to me?" You do not want to put a question mark where God has put a period. Have faith and trust in God. Psalm 56:3 (NIV) says, "When I am afraid, I put my trust in [God]."

You can't allow one bad moment or one bad season to affect the rest of your life. Quit reliving the hurt. Quit replaying the recording of what that person said and did to you. It's time to move forward, and the way you move forward is by faith. Believe that God is working all things out for your good. Romans 8:28 (NIV) says, "And we know that in all things God works for the good of those who love him, who have been called according to his purpose." You must decide to get out of that broken place. You may say, "What place? Why did this happen to me? Things never go right for me." Move into your new place of blessing and favor. Say to yourself, "I am enough. I am worthy. I am God's work of art."

Thought for the Day

Learn to move forward. Accept what is, let go of what was, and have faith in what will be.

Letting Your Light Shine

How you live your life sends a message to others. It's not really about what you say—it is more about what you do. When you smile, are kind and respectful, and love others, you send out a light. When you understand that your life is a light, you cannot be full of complaints and negativity. When you start out your day, make sure you are shining your light on all the things around you. Do this when you are in traffic, driving to your job, or talking to your friends, family, and companions. If you are complaining and being negative, there is no way for that light to shine. The real power is in you.

You are an illuminator. When you are around people, your attitude and smile should illuminate that room. Instead of complaining or being negative, we should ask God to help our light to shine: "God, help me become a better influencer." Matthew 5:16 (NIV) says, "Let your light shine before others, that they may see your good deeds and glorify your Father in heaven." Don't complain about where God has put you. God has you exactly where you need to be, and your light has a purpose.

That boss who gives you a hard time. Shine your light. That co-worker has a bad attitude. Shine your light. That driver who thinks they're the only person on the road. Shine your light. That family member you don't like to be around. Shine your light. The darker the situation, the brighter your light will shine; so keep smiling, keep being nice, keep being respectful. Light will always overcome darkness. Light is designed to work in darkness. God will send you into dark places so that you can make a difference.

Think first! Before you start praying people out of your life, you may be the light that God sent into that person's life. Something to think about: you can't see light in a lighted place; light is meant to be seen in darkness. Jesus didn't hang out in church. Jesus was criticized for being around sinners and outcasts, such as tax collectors, the poor, and the sick. Jesus was letting his light shine. Many of those people became believers. People will believe a sermon that they see more than a sermon they hear.

More than anything, our light should shine in our homes. As adults, we can tell our children and young people about being respectful, but if they see us being disrespectful and dishonest, it will go in one ear and out the other. So go out and be the light in this dark world.

Thought for the Day

Don't allow others to diminish your light due to their own fears and insecurities. Instead, let your light shine so brightly that you illuminate a pathway for others to find their way out of the darkness.

Keep Your Joy

We all can become frustrated and upset when we are caught in traffic, when someone is rude to us, or when things in our lives aren't working out. Life is full of inconvenience and disappointment. We can't stop things from happening; the key is to know how you are going to handle it. No one can take your joy, so that means you are in control of your joy. The only way someone can have your joy is if you give it away. Don't give away your joy. The reason some people are not happy is because they are constantly giving away their joy. They become frustrated and upset about things they have no control over, like being stuck in traffic, standing in a long line at the supermarket, someone being rude to them, or someone not speaking to them.

You must make up your mind that you are going to have a good day. Quit letting the same people and things upset you. You must understand where your joy comes from. Our joy is rooted in who God is. True joy can be obtained in heartfelt gratitude for God's love, mercy, and grace. Our joy is not about worldly possessions and accomplishments. Those things are temporal. Romans 15:13 (NIV) says, "May the God of hope fill you with all joy and peace as you trust in him, so that you may overflow with hope by the power of the Holy Spirit." The Bible says that the source of our joy is Jesus, and the joy of the Lord is our strength. Life is too short to live in constant frustration; don't allow people's negativity to steal your joy. Get rid of the joy stealers in your life, and God will send you the right people to be in your life.

Thought for the Day

Joy does not simply happen to us; we must choose joy and keep choosing it every day.

Moving Forward

It's easy to look back over your life and think about what didn't work out and who wronged you. You may say to yourself, "If only I finished school." "If only I listened to my parents." "If only I hadn't hooked up with the wrong person." Focusing on the past will keep you from the great future that God has for you. You must let go of what didn't work out. Let go of the hurt, pain, and disappointments. Accept that you cannot change the past; however, you can start shaping your future.

Let go of the negative experience—whether it occurred twenty years ago or twenty minutes ago—and move forward. Do not bring yesterday's baggage into your today because it will poison your future. Don't allow your past to be used as a reason why you are not moving forward. Do not allow bad relationships, a nasty divorce, betrayal, or a difficult childhood to keep you from moving forward. God wants to increase your life. Don't get stuck on the negative things that happened to you. Learn to walk lighter. Let go of the baggage. When you fly on an airplane, heavy baggage always costs extra, and this is also true in life.

Start every morning fresh and renewed and do not live in regret. Focus on what you can change, not what you cannot. Develop a "what's done is done" mindset and quit living life in the rearview mirror. Automakers make the rearview mirror small and the windshield big for a reason. Where you are headed is much more important than what you've left behind. Stay in faith and quit mourning what has been lost. Stop talking about what happened to you. Stop replaying it over and over in your mind. Stop reliving it. Change the channel, allow yourself to heal, and see what God has for your future.

Thought for the Day

You can't start the next chapter of your life if you keep rereading your last one.

You Are God's Work of Art

There are times when we feel that we are not adequate. Some people say if they were taller, they would do this, or if they were thinner, they would have more confidence in themselves. Some will even go as far as to wonder if life wouldn't be so hard if they were a different nationality. I'm here to tell you that you are exactly what you need to be. You are the right nationality and the right height and size—you are perfect just the way you are because you are His work of art. Ephesians 2:10 (AMP) says, "For we are His workmanship [His own master work, a work of art], created in Christ Jesus for good works, which God prepared [for us] beforehand."

You must believe you are a work of art. You are special and uniquely made by the hands of God. Do not wait for someone else to tell you that you are a work of art, that you are special. Belief starts on the inside. Psalm 139:14 (NIV) says, "I praise you because I am fearfully and wonderfully made; your works are wonderful, I know that full well."

No matter what you see about yourself, God sees His work of art. We live in a world where the emphasis is on how you look, how you dress, your complexion, and your size. Change your lens about how you see yourself and start seeing yourself as being smart, beautiful, loved, chosen, and God's masterpiece.

Don't be a critic. Criticizing yourself is not being humble, it is being hurtful. Stop speaking death over yourself and start speaking life. You are a work of art with divine purpose. If you believe you are a work of art, you will feel like you are. We are the light, and our light represents Jesus. We are created for the purpose of action. The purpose of light is to shine in darkness. Our job is to shine and share.

We have a responsibility to tell others about Jesus. How a person describes themselves says a lot about how they see themselves. Do you tell others that you are a moody person? Do you find yourself criticizing yourself and others? How do people feel when they are in your presence? How would you describe your personality? Are you more focused on the inside of you or the outside?

Thought for the Day

Each one of us is God's special work of art. Through us, He teaches, inspires, delights, encourages, informs, and uplifts all those who view our lives.

Chapter 6

You Are a Champion

The Pursuit of Happiness

Everyone desires to be happy in their lives. You want to be happy in your marriage, with your children, in your job, and with your finances. Being happy is something we all pursue in our lives. Many people will do just about anything to be happy. There's nothing wrong with working toward something that will make you happy, but we must make sure our pursuit is in the right place.

What is happiness? The *Webster Ninth Collegiate Dictionary* says happiness is a state of well-being and contentment. Happiness can vary from one person to another. When people talk about happiness, they are talking about how they feel in the present moment. If your bills are paid, your home life is good, and your job is going well, people assume that natural things will make you happy. You won't find happiness in money, a career, or people, because all those things come and go. The only source of true happiness is in the Lord. The things you receive in your life that give you happiness are because you believe in God. John 15:11 (KJV) says, "These things have I spoken unto you, that my joy might remain in you, and that your joy might be full." Signs of happiness include:

- Feeling like you are living the life you wanted.
- Going with the flow and being willing to take life as it comes.
- Enjoying positive, healthy relationships with other people.
- Feeling satisfied with your life.
- Being open to new ideas and experiences.
- Practicing self-care and treating yourself with kindness and compassion.
- Wanting to share your happiness and joy with others.

Why is it important to be happy? Scientific evidence suggests that being happy may have major benefits for your life. Being happy promotes a healthy lifestyle. Laughing is good medicine, and smiling puts you in a good mood. Being positive helps combat stress. Happiness boosts your immune system, protects your heart, and reduces pain. How do you find happiness? Philippians 4:11 (KJV) says, "Not that I speak in respect of want for I have learned, in whatsoever state I am, therewith to be content." Being content means being satisfied with what you have. Happiness means being content; recognizing you are special, loved, uniquely made, and chosen by God; and loving yourself. You can't love others unless you love yourself.

Thought for the Day

Be happy, not because everything is good but because you can see the good in everything.

No More Excuses

It is easy to come up with a reason for why we can't accomplish our dreams, why we can't be happy, and why we can't overcome problems. Excuses are a crutch that people use to explain why they are still at the same place in their life. Excuses are used to justify why they can't get to work on time or why no one gave them a break. When you continue to make excuses, you will justify where you are. Excuses give you permission to settle: "I didn't finish school." "I'm not qualified for that position at my job." "I don't have a degree." You have the power to overcome anything in your life, but the first thing you must do is get rid of the excuses. If you continue to blame your job, what you don't have, your husband/wife, or your nationality, you are going to be stuck. It's time for you to step into a new level.

Have a no-more-excuses attitude. Decide for yourself that you are going to be happy and stop making excuses for why you can't be happy. There are no more excuses for giving up on your dreams. Second Peter 1:3 (NIV) says, "His divine power has given us everything we need for a godly life through our knowledge of him who called us by his own glory and goodness." Success is already inside you. You have exactly what you need to be successful. Stop looking at what others have because God gave you everything you need to accomplish your goals, dreams, desires, and ministry. Start running your own race. You are gifted, talented, smart, uniquely designed, and qualified. Your excuses are holding you back from reaching your destiny. When God is ready to take you to a new level, get rid of excuses.

Thought for the Day

Success occurs when your dreams get bigger than your excuses.

Faith under Construction

We all experience difficult times. You may have experienced doors closing, plans that didn't turn out the way you hoped, a job situation that didn't get better, or a bad health report. It seems as if things are not getting better. Although you are praying and waiting, nothing has changed. Waiting on God can be very difficult. A person can become discouraged while waiting for their situation to change. The million-dollar question is, what do you do in the process of waiting? Stay encouraged. God knows what you need, and He has heard your prayers. Find that scripture that will fortify and strengthen you throughout the day.

Why is it important to stay encouraged? Encouragement grows confidence and gives you a reason to focus on positive attempts and ignore negative ones. The lack of encouragement in one's life can cause discouragement. Discouragement will deprive you of your hope, confidence, and faith. Isaiah 40:31 (KJV) says, "But they that wait upon the Lord shall renew their strength; they shall mount up with wings as eagles; they shall run, and not be weary; and they shall walk, and not faint." God will use your problems to push you. God will use your trials to train you.

Mustard Seed Faith is discussed in Matthew 17:20. Jesus specifically chose to reference the mustard seed because he knew the characteristic that the seed possessed. It is resilient. It is totally unaffected by its surroundings. No matter what's happening in the garden, the mustard seed stays true to itself and continues to grow.

Faith is necessary in the lives of believers. The Word says, "Without faith, it is impossible to please God" (Hebrews 11:6 [NIV]). Faith is not believing God can, it's knowing that He will.

How do you put your faith under construction? Make time for God throughout your day. Everything begins and ends with God.

Give the situation over to God and leave it there. Speak faith-filled words to encourage yourself: "I am the righteousness of Christ." "I am more than a conqueror." "I am loved, chosen, blessed, and victorious." See your situation from faith-filled eyes. No matter what is going on around you, see the result you desire and put your faith into practice. Faith grows when you are tested, and your faith increases when you use it.

Thought for the Day

Faith is like a muscle; it only grows when you use it. Need stronger faith? Test it like you test your strength. Neglect it, and it will weaken.

Your Blessing Is Already Inside You

Many of us find ourselves doing some sort of self-improvement, looking for ways to improve and reinvent ourselves. There's nothing wrong with improving yourself, but if you look deep down inside of you and take time to recognize what God has put inside you, then you will stop looking around and realize you already have it in you. We pray and ask God for specific things in our life when we already have the potential and power inside us to get whatever we need in our lives. First John 4:4 (KJV) says, "Ye are of God, little children, and have overcome them: because greater is he that is in you, than he that is in the world." When you recognize the greatness inside of you, you can possess all that God has promised you. There were times I came up against obstacles in my life and ask God to reveal what's inside of me to overcome these obstacles. By doing this, God also showed me the resources I had available to help me overcome these challenges and guide me to my destiny. God answers prayers! I don't live my life in doubt, fear and second guessing myself any longer. Now I recognize the blessing is inside of me.

Thought for the Day

I'm blessed with everything I need. I am working hard toward everything I want. And most of all, I appreciate and thank God for what I have.

Starting Your Day with God on Your Mind

How you start your day is important. When you get up in the morning and you have already decided that your day is going to be a bad day—such as complaining about your boss and coworker or the traffic before you even get in your car—you have set the tone for the rest of your day. Having a positive mindset will start your day in the right direction. The right mindset will have you thinking and speaking positively throughout your day. Start your day with God on your mind and make time for God. Why? It is important to God. We were created to have relationship and fellowship with God. He wants to hear from you because He cares about what goes on in your life.

God cares about everything that is connected to you, such as your job, your family, and your health. He cares about your goals and desires. Be intentional in making time for God. When you get up in the morning, say, "Good morning, God. Thank you for waking me up." Before you turn on your car, say a prayer. Before you make a major decision, consult with God. Show an attitude of gratitude for God. When you start your morning with God, it will put you in a good mood while enabling you to be confident and enjoy new success.

Don't allow things like having a bad attitude and complaining to keep you separated from God. Stay in fellowship with God. Prayer opens the way for God to work. Prayer is the avenue we use to give God all our cares and to thank Him for His protection, provision, and love. Give your day to God. Ask God, "Who can I bless today? How can I make a difference in my job?"

Thought for the Day

Morning is God's way of telling us, "Here is one more time!" Live life. Make a difference. Touch hearts. Inspire a soul. Encourage the mind. Good morning.

You Are Treasured

We can go through life without valuing ourselves. It could be because you may not have graduated from college and didn't get that degree. You may not have a fancy job or live in a big house. You can walk away feeling not good enough. We tend to attach our value to things in order to feel special and worthy about ourselves. We tell children to go to school and learn so they can obtain knowledge and accomplish great things in life. In doing this, no one can take away that knowledge that is inside of them. If we look at this as a child of God, once we give ourselves to Christ, God's spirit comes inside of us and we have His power in us called the Holy Spirit, our hidden treasure.

Hidden treasure is something of great value that has not been revealed, or maybe the owner doesn't know its worth. It is vitally important that you know your worth and value. Your worth doesn't come from man or this world. Your worth comes from God, the one that created you, the one that sent His Son, Jesus, to die for you. "But God commendeth His love toward us, in that, while we were yet sinners, Christ died for us" (Rom. 5:8 [KJV].

I have seen television shows where someone had a valuable item in their home, and they did not know its worth. Someone then comes along and recognizes its worth and value. What makes this person understand the worth of that item? Is it their experience, knowledge, or background that makes them qualified to recognize the value of something? Yes!

It also takes all of that to understand and recognize the worth you have inside of you. The good news is that God has given us His spirit to help us along the way. "But we have this treasure in jars of clay to show that this all-surpassing power is from God and not from us" (2 Cor. 4:7 [NIV]). Understand that in all actuality, it is not about the outside—it is all about the inside, God's precious Spirit, and the great message of His Son. That is the precious treasure we must find within ourselves.

How does this treasure get hidden in the first place? Treasures are buried deep, and something that is buried for a long time can be hidden for various reasons. We all have been through tough times in our lives. It doesn't matter if you are a Christian or not, you will experience difficulties, discouragement, bad news, or bad relationships, if not all these things. Hard times have no respect for a person. These experiences can cause your treasure to get buried and hidden in your life. There is good news: you can defeat and overcome those things with the Spirit of God, which will help you rediscover that hidden treasure. In you, God has deposited greatness, gifts, and talents, as well as His power and His love.

Thought for the Day

Self-worth comes from one thing: thinking that you are worthy.

Chapter 7

The New You

Take Your Hands Off

I think most people feel that they are patient until they find themselves in a situation. An example is when someone on the road cuts you off, or a person at the supermarket checkout is not going fast enough because you are in a rush. I'm sure we can all identify with one or both of those things. It is when we are put to the test that we realize we are not as patient as we think we are. Being patient in the waiting process can be very trying, especially when you are waiting for God to show up. In these situations, we have asked ourselves, "Where is God?" Because at the end of the day, we want what we want right now.

What time is it? It's God time. God's time is different from our time. "With the Lord a day is like a thousand years, and a thousand years are like a day" (2 Pet. 3:8 [NIV]. Don't panic. God is not going to take that long to answer your prayer. Asking God for the patience, endurance, and faith to wait is always a good thing. Waiting is demonstrated by active dependence on God. God uses waiting as an opportunity to strengthen our faith, trust, and reliance on Him. God is never late. He's always right on time. I know many of you have said, "I prayed for something, and God didn't come through." But remember, God's timing is perfect!

I have learned that God will give us what we need, not what we want. He knows what's best for us. Maybe:
- You weren't ready for that job just yet.
- You weren't ready for that relationship yet.
- God had to remove some people from your life.

Maybe God allowed you to go through that tough time to strengthen your faith so you would learn to trust and rely on Him. There will be obstacles and people that come up against you. It is only through the course of time that things are matured, revealed, and made ready. How many of us know that when things don't go as quickly as we'd like, we feel we need to help God out and put our hand on it? You see, God can get things to us a lot quicker if we take our hands off.

Psalm 46:10 (NIV) says, "Be still, and know that I am God." Patience is not one of our virtues naturally. We must learn how to be patient and let God work out His will in our lives. In the Bible we learn that Sarah had a problem with being still and waiting on God. She was barren and wanted a child. God had told Abraham and Sarah that she would have a child, but Sarah felt God was taking too long, so she asked her husband, Abraham, to bear a child with her maidservant. "Go in unto my maid; it may be that I may obtain children by her" (Gen. 16:2 [KJV]).

Putting your hands on something that God has already put into motion can change and shift the very thing that God has set in place. Be still! We all can agree that when we don't get things in our time, we feel that God needs our help because He is not moving fast enough. Some of you feel that time is running out and you are getting older. You are waiting for God to move in specific areas of your life such as getting married, finding a new home, starting a business, or going back to school.

I'm here to tell you that it's never too late. When God's hands are on it, there is a blessing attached to it. Learning to be patient is one of the fruits of the spirit (see Galatians 5:22). Let God work things out for you. What God has for you is for you. "God is not a man, that he should lie; neither the son of man, that he should repent: hath he said, and shall he not do it?" (Num. 23:19 [KJV]).

Thought for the Day

God will fight your battles if you just keep still. He can carry you through. Trust Him. Keep standing, keep believing, and keep hoping.

Keep Speaking Victory

Your words are setting the direction for your life. If you want to know what you are going to be like five years from now, listen to what you are saying about yourself. If you are saying things like "I am never going to get married;" "I'm never going to get out of debt;" "I'm never going to own my own home;" "That child is never going to get right;" you are prophesying into your future. Pay attention to what you say. You can't speak defeat and have victory. You will eat the fruit of your words. Pay attention to what you say about your health, finances, children, marriage, ministry, and business. Proverbs 18:21 (KJV) says, "Death and life are in the power of the tongue: and they that love it shall eat the fruit thereof."

You will become what you continually say, and that's why it's important to continually to speak victory over your life. There is so much negativity going on in the world; you must make sure that it doesn't affect your mind. Start speaking victory words: "I am strong." "I am smart." "I am qualified." "I have the favor of God." "I am chosen." "I am the righteous of Christ." "I am loved by God." "I am blessed." "I am fearfully and wonderfully made." "I am created in the image and likeness of God." "I can do great things in my life." The fruit of those words are life and blessing, and we give life to the words by speaking them out. Decide not to complain and start turning the negativity into praise:

"God, thank you for good health."
"Thank you for your favor in my life."
"Thank you for never leaving me or forsaking me."
"Thank you for going and making the crooked places straight."

"God, thank you for my family, finances, job, ministry, and health."

Don't invite defeated words into your life. Don't say that your situation will never get better, your child will never change, you're not going to get that job, or you're never going to get that degree. Change your old message and start recording a new message. Words that go out of your mouth can take root in your heart. Are you sending your words in the right direction? When you talk defeat, that is the road you will travel. Start speaking victory over your own life. Don't wait for someone else to tell you good things.

Thought for the Day

Victory is not the absence of problems; it is the presence of power.

A Transformed Life

We are living in a world where being busy has become the new normal. If I ask how your day is going, you will start running down your entire day and it is not even noon. We live in a technological time that should make our lives easier, but it hasn't. As a matter of fact, it seems like people don't have time for anything productive and meaningful anymore. Don't allow the things in this world to consume your time and mind. Stop looking at Facebook to see how many likes you have and spend less time taking selfies. Don't allow technology to conform you but allow God to transform your life.

    A transformed life leaves time to study the Word of God, pray, and work on yourself. It is important to continue to change and grow so that we can become better parents, spouses, individuals, and men and women of God. Matthew 5:13–14 [NIV] "You are the salt of the earth. But if the salt loses it saltiness, how can it be made salty again? It is no longer good for anything, except to be thrown out and trampled underfoot. You are the light of the world. A town built on a hill cannot be hidden."

    How can we be the light of the world when our bulb is low? How can we be the salt of the earth when we are walking around bland with no love and no zeal for God? Your Spirit must be refreshed for God to get the best out of you. If we can be honest with ourselves, some of us need to jump-start our spirituality. This refresh comes by renewing your mind, spending quality time with God, reading His word, and allowing the Word of God to transform your life. When your mind is renewed, you will experience transformation. To have a transformed life, you must let go of your old mindset of negativity. Let go of fear, unforgiveness, and shame. You must embrace the

Word of God, "meditate on [the scripture] day and night" (Josh. 1:8 [NIV]), "keep a song in [your] mouth" (Ps. 40:3 [NIV]), and thank God throughout the day for you family, health, job, etc. The Word of God will replenish, restore, resuscitate, and revitalize.

A transformed mind will experience a transformed life. When a real transformation takes place, there is no way you can go back to your old self. A transformed mind has a different outlook. A transformation-minded person will treat people differently and will not be easily knocked down because they know who they are. They will not see themselves as a victim but a victor. Romans 12:2 (NIV) says, "Do not conform to the pattern of this world but be transformed by the renewing of your mind." We should act and look different from the world. Your behavior should not be like the world; your communication should be different. "Bad company corrupts good character" (1 Cor. 15:33 [NIV]). We should treat one another differently. Matthew 22:36–37 tells us to love God and one another, which is the greatest commandment.

Thought for the Day

Nothing gets transformed in your life until your mind is transformed.

Pushed into Your Purpose

I believe most of us are uncomfortable when being pushed to a place that is unfamiliar. A place that may challenge us, a place of uncertainty. When you are pushed, you may not understand the reason and purpose behind it, but if God's hands are on it, then it will work out for your good. God is not as concerned with our comfort as He is with our purpose. We all will experience difficulties, but God will use those difficult experiences to push us. It may be the loss of a job, finances, or a marriage; the betrayal of a friend or a loved one; or abandonment.

God doesn't cause those things, but He will use them to move us to change. God is not trying to make our lives miserable; He is pushing us into our purpose. You will experience closed doors. Every closed door is not a bad thing. Every person who walked away from you is not a mistake. God understands that we wouldn't go without a push. When people are comfortable with the way things are in their life, they will not move unless they are stretched out of their comfort zone. This could be in finding new friends or in taking risks like starting a new career, going back to school, or trying a new hobby. In many cases, if God doesn't close doors, we will never move from where we are. God does those things to help us grow. Every difficult and bad break wasn't meant to stop you—it was meant to push you, mature you, and make you stronger.

Every push, every difficulty, every uncomfortable situation you experienced has deposited something inside of you and has made you who you are today. You wouldn't be prepared for the new level if you had not gone through those things. Don't complain about what you lost; it will all work out for the good. Romans 8:28 (KJV) says,

"And we know that all things work together for good to them that love God, to them who are the called according to his purpose."

Develop a new perspective that these things are not meant to stop you but to promote you. It may be uncomfortable but know that God is using it to push you to a new level; He's pushing you into greater things that are pushing you into your purpose.

Step into your new season. Don't complain about what you lost. Accept the new. God will send the right people into your life, and He will promote you.

Thought for the Day

Push harder than yesterday if you want a different tomorrow.

Chapter 8

You Are Valued

Recognizing What You Have

There are times when we focus so much on what we don't have that we miss out on what God is doing in our lives right now. You have everything you need inside of you and all around you to be successful and to fulfill your God-given purpose. Everything that has been assigned and meant for you, is inside of you.

God did not create you with just enough; He created you with more than enough. We are created in the image and likeness of God, so if we are the image of God, I think it is safe to say that we have all that we need to be great. In John 14:12, Jesus tells his disciples that they will do greater work. Look past what you think is ordinary because God specializes in the extraordinary. What you must do is recognize and identify what you do have, and the answer is inside of you. God will always use something that you already have. You don't have to look to someone else for it. You don't have to attempt to buy or fabricate it because it is already inside of you.

It has always been there; you just didn't realize it. Moses didn't think he had what it took to lead the Israelites to the Promised Land, but he did. David had what it took to be king, but his own father didn't see it. That is why people can't determine your destiny.

The solution is inside of you. It may look small; it may look like there's not much to it, but trust what God put inside of you. You must know that many of us have talked ourselves out of dreams and opportunities. You may be that person who feels like you don't have the time, you don't have the resources, and you don't have what it takes. What I say to that is yes, you do!

Prayer for Recognizing

God, help me to recognize the people you put in my life. Help me to see the ideas and resources that will help guide me to my destiny. God, open my eyes so I can see what I have inside of me and what's at my disposal. Amen.

Thought for the Day

Everything you need is already inside of you. Don't wait for others to light your fire. You have your own matches.

Bringing Value to Your Relationships

Studies say that people who have healthy relationships are more likely to feel happier and satisfied with their lives. They are less likely to have physical and mental health problems. Healthy relationships can increase your sense of worth and belonging and help you feel less alone. To bring value to your relationships, you must understand that relationships (such as those with your parents, children, friends, siblings, etc.) in your life are valuable. Not all relationships are created equal; however, some people in your life can be challenging, but if you value the relationship, then it's worth working through.

Balancing the people in your life is up to you, including identifying good relationships from bad relationships. Bad relationships are with those who are constantly disrespectful, dishonest, disloyal, critical, and negative. I have come to realize that every relationship serves a purpose, and I believe you can grow and learn from every relationship you have been in. Relationships with people in your life are meant to be enjoyed, not cause frustration. Find the good and worth in that relationship and focus on the positive things about that person, not the negative things.

Remember, no one is perfect, including you. Allow love to be your guide and compass. Love allows us to look at people from a different lens, not through the lens of judgment and condemnation. Love allows us to forgive easily and quickly, and it doesn't keep track. God doesn't record our mistakes. "I will forgive their wickedness and will remember their sins no more" (Heb. 8:12 [NIV]).

By bringing value to your relationships, you will have joy, peace, happiness, and contentment, and you will have no frustration.

Thought for the Day

We can improve our relationships with others by leaps and bounds if we become encouragers instead of critics.

Put Your Reputation in God's Hands

We all have a desire to have a good reputation. We know how important it is. I have heard people say, "Your reputation precedes you." Having a good reputation can open doors and cause the right people to come into your life. Proverbs 22:1 (KJV) says, "A good name is rather to be chosen than great riches." When others try to come and tarnish your reputation, slander your name, or start rumors, what you must do is put your reputation in God's hands. Let God defend you. Many of us want to defend ourselves, so we will want to give that person a piece of our mind, but the scriptures say to guard our heart, not our reputation.

It is not your job to guard your reputation; leave it to God. If you try to do it, you will wear yourself out because if you try to silence that person, there will be someone else right behind them. God knows how to cause you to be seen in the right way. God knows how to change the minds of those around you and silence the negative voices. Let God do it His way. He may not stop what they are doing, and He may not shut them up; however, God will have you shine during this time. God will promote you while they are still talking; He will honor you right in front of them and lift you up while they are trying to push you down. God is your defender, so don't allow people to stir you up, and don't get thrown into a conflict.

Jesus was not concerned about his reputation. "[Jesus] made himself of no reputation" (Phil. 2:7 [KJV]), and people still slandered him. He was judged, accused, and mocked. Jesus did not spend his time defending his reputation, as he had a greater purpose.

Thought for the Day

If you focus on your character, God will take care of your reputation.

About the Author

Michele Luckey, being born and raised in New Brunswick, NJ has always had a love and desire to know God. Michele accepted the Lord at an early age and has been serving God her entire life. Michele answered the call of God in 1996 and was licensed and ordained at True Servant Worship & Praise Church. In 2003, her husband, Bishop David Luckey, Jr., and Pastor Michele founded Without Walls Church. Pastor Michele oversees many ministries at Without Walls Church, but her passion is heading the Women & Youth Ministry. Pastor Michele preaches the Word of God which brings healing and deliverance to the people of God. Pastor Michele also founded and leads a podcast called Morning Inspiration. Morning Inspiration was created to help people start their day in a positive manner, giving inspirational words through encouragement based on the word of God. Pastor Michele is a certified Florist, and has also launched her business in 2023, called Michele's Seasonal & Event Designs.

Pastor Michele shares an education business with her husband where they have helped students in the areas of academics servicing the New York, New Jersey areas for over 20 years.

Pastor Michele lives in Somerset, NJ with her husband, Bishop David Luckey Jr. Michele and David have been married for 36 years and from that union they are blessed with three children and seven grandchildren. Pastor Michele's greatest joy is being a grandmother (Me-Mom) to her grandchildren.

www.ingramcontent.com/pod-product-compliance
Lightning Source LLC
LaVergne TN
LVHW051956060526
838201LV00059B/3675